Planning & Running Your Exhibition Stand

A practical guide to getting the most out of exhibitions

Nathan Hoshen

Management Update

First published in Great Britain in 1988 by Management
Update Ltd., 99a Underdale Road, Shrewsbury SY2 5EE
Shropshire, United Kingdom. (Telephone 0743 232556)

ISBN 0 946679 29 0

978   4

Typesetting by Litho Link Ltd., Leighton, Welshpool,
Powys, Wales.
Printed and bound in England by Billings Ltd., Worcester.

Planning & Running Your Exhibition Stand

A practical guide to getting the most out of exhibitions

Contents

Acknowledgements

The publishers are grateful to Industrial and Trade Fairs Ltd., a member of the Association of Exhibition Organisers, for permission to reproduce items from their exhibition manuals.

Our thanks also go to Christina de la Mare for her illustrations.

Introduction

The number and variety of exhibitions and trade fairs held have been growing rapidly in recent years. Each year new exhibitions are launched — both at home and over-seas — presenting the would be exhibitor with a wide and bewildering choice.

Whilst doubts are often expressed about the tangible results of taking part in exhibitions they can offer the potential exhibitor an extremely effective means of prom-oting products or services and expanding the existing customer base *provided* they are properly planned and managed.

Exhibiting is never easy — it is always hard and often exhausting work for all those involved, but if close attention is paid to all the elements which contribute to successful exhibitions they can be rewarding and cost effective.

Success depends in part on choosing the best exhibition for your purpose and then selecting the ideal location for your stand. However, these and other elements are of little help if they are not supported by well-motivated, trained and efficient staff. You need staff who know your business inside out and can field any questions about the products and services you offer. You also need to ensure that your staff know how to handle enquiries, behave courteously to customers and are experienced negotiators. Of course, it does not end there: you also need an attractive and well-designed stand and the right kind of literature.

This book offers the exhibitor advice and guidelines on all aspects of exhibitions from planning to dismantling a stand. It has been written with the inclusion of many checklists so as to provide concise and helpful information based on experience gained over many years. It will help the newcomer to plan and run an effective stand for the first time. It will also be found useful to those who wish to review their exhibition policies and plans or examine some aspects of the exhibiting process in greater detail.

1. Defining your Market

You can't begin to promote your products effectively or develop a sound marketing strategy — let alone consider taking part in an exhibition — unless you have carefully researched the market place and established which particular markets or market segments you are going to concentrate on. This holds true for domestic as well as overseas sales, but is particualry important when you are thinking of taking an exhibition stand overseas for the first time.

As this is not a book about marketing in general, but exhibitions in particular, we will concentrate here on some of the key issues which you should be thinking about if you are considering selling and exhibiting your products abroad.

Of course, many of the issues raised apply not just to defining overseas markets but we are assuming that you are familiar with your domestic market and have your sales and marketing strategies already well-developed for exploiting this. It is when you are thinking of expanding exports and perhaps considering a stand of an overseas exhibition for the first time that serious problems can emerge. You will require an additional range of management skills and know-how plus a clear set of marketing objectives if you are to succeed overseas. You need to be very clear about what you want to achieve in the medium and longer term before plunging into overseas exhibitions.

A starting point is to ask yourself such questions as:

1. Has domestic demand slowed down?

2. Do you have new or under-utilised production capacity?

3. Have you fully exploited the potential domestic market and now wish to exploit your investment in people, buildings, production know-how, etc., by overseas sales?

4. Have you found a gap in the overseas market for your products? Can they readily be presented or adapted so as to meet customer needs?

5. Is now the right time to be thinking about developing export activities? Why?

6. Are you motivated in part by the challenge of developing new trading links and widening your business horizons?

7. Do you have any firm evidence to indicate that there are untapped opportunities for production and marketing collaboration with foreign companies? Could such contacts lead to new product development?

8. Have sales enquiries from abroad increased in recent times, suggesting that there is an on-going demand for your product abroad?

In devising an export strategy you should have four main aims in the back of your mind:

1. PROFITABILITY

You must be realistic about pricing and discount policies. Both individual as well as groups of products should all be contributing to profits. You should also ensure that your total sales mix both at home and abroad is contributing to overall profits.

2. EXPANSION

You must be really serious about trying to expand your market beyond the narrow confines of domestic sales. Will your new sales efforts be matched by enhanced administrative, staff, production, quality control, etc., resources? Can you effectively deal with the increased volume of business? Do your staff have the necessary skills and exporting 'know-how'?

3. SPREADING RISKS

In exporting you should be seeking to spread your business risks. This can be expressed in two ways:

a. by trying to maintain a certain ratio of home to overseas sales. Remember that home sales generally cover most of the fixed costs of running the business, whilst exports tend to be based on variable costs. The higher the ratio of exports to total sales, the more fixed costs can be allocated to them. If, for example, exports constitute 90 per cent of total sales revenue, all fixed costs can be allocated and recovered in the export prices but if exports make up only 30 per cent of all sales, then the full amount of fixed costs can be primarily allocated and recovered from home sales.

b. by trying to maintain a certain ratio of export sales amongst a number of countries. Overseas markets can be volatile and you should not be putting all 'your eggs' in one export market! In trying to spread your risks (and opportunities) make a point of trying to export to a number of different markets.

4. CONCENTRATING EFFORT

Remember that Pareto's law tends to apply to overseas sales as well as other business activities. There is plenty of evidence to show that in practice around 80 per cent of exports tend to be concentrated in 20 per cent of countries: the remaining 20 per cent or so are likely to be distributed amongst 80 per cent of overseas markets.

As you probably have limited resources, it is important to concentrate them on, say, two or three target countries (or perhaps two or three large cities abroad). The initial response you receive should help you decide where you should be focussing your efforts in the future.

In choosing the target market(s) for your products it is suggested that you go about this systematically as follows:

a. Initial Selection

Choose fifteen countries which for geographical, economic, political and social reasons are likely to prove practical and profitable markets. Collect the necessary background data remembering that in the larger countries each major city should itself be regarded as a target area. The USA, for example, is a huge country with a number of target states and cities: it should not be regarded as just one large market.

b. Selection at the Product Stage

Out of the initial fifteen countries chosen, pick (say) ten which you consider are suitable for your products taking into account the size of the market, its stage of development and growth trends in recent years within the context of import, customs and quality standard constraints.

c. Reducing the list still further

Of the ten remaining countries, states or cities, pick (say) the five most likely to meet the following criteria:

• Profitability targets

- Those which suit your range of products
- Ease of market penetration from a marketing and financial point of view
- Readily available and reliable market information
- Your own business judgement

d. Final Selection

Finally reduce your list to just three markets (countries, states or cities) which you think are most likely to offer the best prospects of success in the immediate future. Visit one or two of them to make sure that you really have made the right selection and check:

- Market acceptability of your product(s)
- Local marketing channels in more depth
- Packaging and price levels
- Local agents or representatives (appointing one when you have carefully examined what is available)
- Whether there is scope for other forms of co-operation in the marketing or production of your products

You should, after your visit, be in a position to have a more detailed and accurate picture of the prospects and your future strategy. Concentrate most of your efforts during the initial year on one or two of the target markets. Once you have drafted a detailed plan and budget and had the broad strategy accepted, you will need to devote some resources to promotion and advertising: you may even be in a position to consider taking space at a local exhibition!

The following checklist will help you to choose the right target market for your products (or services):

COLLECT KEY INFORMATION ABOUT YOUR PRODUCTS

- Do you have a special and new product compared to others available?

- Write down the technical advantages.
- Write down its practical advantages (eg. economical, durable, easy to use, etc.).
- Write down its marketing advantages (eg. easy to store and to transport, attractively priced, etc.).
- Which needs does it meet in the local market?
- Who are the key buyers and what are the main reasons for buying?
- Write down the export advantages (eg. weight, price, high added value, etc.).
- Specify the packaging advantages (eg. durability or attractive design, etc.).
- Does the current production stage justify participation at the exhibition? A product under development should not be exhibited: it is too early to exhibit any item which you cannot supply in significant quantities!
- Compare your products with competing products in your own country and abroad: what are your competitors' products advantages and disadvantages?
- Have your products been tested by a standards institute in your own country or abroad? Collect the findings in writing.
- Can you obtain written recommendations from users in your own country or from abroad?

COLLECT INFORMATION ABOUT TARGET MARKETS LOCALLY USING DESK RESEARCH

a. Collect information about (say) five selected markets: from these choose your target country for your activities during the next year:

- Make sure you ask experts and professionals for their opinions and advice, etc.
- Ask importers who have connections with these countries for their comments.
- Try to establish why other exporters in your line of business have succeeded (and failed).

- Inquire from the appropriate officials in government departments for further information on the target countries.
- Collect data from Embassy and market research libraries and from computerised information sources.
- Ask for help from commercial attachés abroad.
- Find out what information is available on trade unions abroad.

b. *The information you collect should include, for example:*

- Customs and import restrictions for your products in the chosen countries.
- What quality and safety standards have to be met in those countries?
- The size of the potential market for your products, including a check on what is currently on offer and the extent of imports.
- Relevant development plans in these countries.
- Breakdown of buyers of your product.
- General economic data about the income, size of the population and its composition, etc.
- The general economic and political situation in the target country.
- What is the inflation and currency exchange situation?
- Investment and foreign currency transfer regulations and restrictions (if any).
- Is the government stable?
- Lists of importers.
- Lists of companies supplying general and professional advice and consultancy.
- Lists of relevant retail chains, specialist shops and distributors, etc.
- Details of exhibitions held in the target countries and when.

Remember that all this type of information is gleaned by reading professional and general literature, from import/ export data provided by official agencies, from surveys of various countries, interviews with people and mailing letters to economic attachés and other representatives abroad.

The picture you obtain will still be incomplete, but it should enable you to identify and select target countries: subsequently you can collect additional information on the spot.

COLLECTING MARKET INFORMATION ABROAD (FIELD SURVEY)

After collecting a maximum of information at home, you are ready to go abroad in order to check one or two markets in the target countries you have chosen.

The following is a suggested work plan. Let us assume that you have decided that Houston, Texas is the target market for your product (after having collected basic information as outlined above).

You decide to visit Houston at a time when an exhibition appropriate to your product range is being held. The planned length of your visit is 10 working days and 2-4 meetings are scheduled per day: this means you will meet with an average of 30 people.

You travel with your products, pamphlets and brochures, prices and a production and supply plan. If you produce an industrial product which cannot easily be transported, then take along some photographs or perhaps a video film and, of course, full technical specifications.

Write down your aims in order of preference, eg:

1. Finding an agent or importer
2. Presenting the product to prospective customers and obtaining reactions
3. Visiting a local exhibition
4. Visiting competing firms

5. Checking storage, despatch and communications facilities
6. Obtaining orders

Secondary aims:

Gather information as follows:

1. Check on customs and standards requirements. Regarding customers you may discover that you need the approval of a local official, or alternatively, that you need authority covering the whole country (eg. all ports in the USA). Regarding standards you may find that you need an examination by the local standards institute before your product can be imported.
2. Check on the size of the market and make an analysis of customers.
3. Check the competitors.
4. Study the marketing distribution channels and outlets.
5. Study the customers' needs.
6. Check on prices and agents' fees.
7. Examine credit terms and forms of payment.
8. Check advertising and sales promotion, methods and alternatives including the purchase of locally distributed professional publications.
9. Get to known *key people* in professional and commercial circles.

Determine whom you are going to visit and what meetings are necessary, eg.:

1. Small and specialised shops
2. Multiple chainstore outlets
3. Local manufacturers
4. Major distributors and stores
5. Interview candidates for appointment as agents
6. Visit the exhibition and meet the organisers

SUGGESTED APPROACH

a. Going up the marketing chain:

Stage A:
Start by visiting the specialist shops and chains — as a *customer*.

Examine shop window displays and make a note of prices and manufacturers (one day).

Stage B:
Set up meetings with 3-4 small specialist shops (one day) and with 2 buyers of a local marketing chain (one day). Present your products, obtain reactions and ask about colour, packaging, supply and despatch. Remember that you are already familiar with competitors' prices and the quality of their products which you studied in Stage A. At the end of the meeting, ask for information and recommendations regarding local distributors and importers. Announce that you wish to contact a local firm so that you can supply your products on time. Although neither the small shopkeeper, nor the owner of the marketing chain, may buy from you directly, their proximity to the final user should provide you with excellent marketing information.

Stage C:
Set up meetings with the recommended distributors (one day). Present your products, obtain reactions and ask questions. Each distributor has connections with a large number of shops and is likely to be familiar with importers.

Obtain recommendations about local importers and agents.

Stage D:
Set up meetings with the recommended importers and agents (one day). You are already familiar with the market for you have compared prices, found out about agents'

commission and have learned all about your competitors. You will impress the importer you are meeting by your familiarity with his market and this gives you an advantage in negotiating. Pass on any views of shops and distributors who were favourably impressed by your products and are prepared to buy them — mention the names of people you met. The importer will realise you have done your homework and he will be inclined to listen to you. If you mention that they have recommended him as a reliable importer who is able to handle your products, you have won sympathy and goodwill, which will stand you in good stead for co-operation between you and the importer in the future.

b. Going down the marketing chain

Stage A:
Try to meet a number of professional people connected with your products. Much will clearly depend on the kind of products you produce but you are likely to find officials from local government, chambers of commerce, trade unions, advertising agencies, trade journals, specialist laboratories and many more helpful.

Your aim is to see whether any of these contacts can suggest or recommend a suitable and reliable importer.

Stage B:
Fix meetings with any recommended importers and after your presentation answer any questions raised. Make a point of checking on the prespective importer's warehousing and maintenance back-up facilities. Find out how many distributors or representatives he has and who his customers are. Ask whether you could go along to a number of his sales visits with him.

If you think you have found the right importer for you, try to obtain an initial order there and then. This will enable you to test the market and sales performance and plan for a formal agreement.

c. Interviewing possible agents

You may feel that advertising for an agent in a local newspaper is worthwhile. Take care about the wording of the advertisement: stress that you are looking for an agent with good warehousing and office facilities. Outline your range of products and specify the kind of outlets you want covered.

Mention that you will be arriving on a given day and will be staying at a hotel (give name, address and telephone number) and will be happy to meet prospective agents during (say) the first week of your visit. Check first with the hotel that they can provide an efficient service of recording names and telephone numbers of all callers so that you can contact people later. If you anticipate a large number of applications it would be better to arrange for written replies to be left with the hotel's receptionist.

Having made your initial selection of likely candidates invite them for interview. Remember you will shortly have to return home and you therefore need to concentrate on selecting the best candidate before you leave if you are to achieve the first goal you set yourself.

You will also need to check the chosen agent's personal and trade references with the appropriate individuals and organisations.

With the first week over, you can now have a break for a rest or go sightseeing or shopping. Make sure you have obtained all the information you can about local conditions. Sit back and re-examine you first week's activities. Go through any notes you took during your visits and meetings and check that you are ready for the second week's activities.

Visiting manufacturers

It is worth setting aside one day during the second week for visits to companies who may be interested in manufacturing components or perhaps ancilliary products for you locally. You may also wish to explore the possibility of finding a manufacturer who may have the facilities and interest in producing your product locally. Remember that most manufacturing companies are not keen on visits from representatives of competitors whether local or from abroad. Your chances of making progress in this field therefore often depend on diplomacy and the way you approach the local company. Whilst manufacturers may not welcome visitors from competitors, they do welcome potential buyers!

Therefore initially make an approach as a buyer who is exploring opportunities to find a local manufacturer of some of your components or ancilliary products. By making contact in this way you are likely to attract interest. If during your meetings with potential manufacturers you feel that there are some which are likely candidates for further co-operation, you can always mention the matter and see how the other party reacts. Such approaches are unlikely to bear immediate results so you must be patient. If it transpires that interest is shown, invite your opposite number to visit you in your country for further talks and negotiations.

Checking on warehousing, despatch and administrative services

You will probably need to devote another day during the second week to reviewing the storage, packing, despatch and communication facilities with the chosen importer or agent. You can find out what methods are employed, what costs are involved and how effective all the ancilliary services are. If the agent is too busy, ask for one of his assistants to go through the procedures, etc., with you.

Obtain reactions from customers if you can to ensure that the services available meet their needs.

Visiting a local Exhibition

Another day in the second week of your visit could be profitably spent in company with your agent at an exhibition. You can pick up a lot of useful information from such an event and obtain valuable advice and guidance from contact with your man on the spot. If your ties develop, you may well be able to consider exhibiting on your agent's stand in future years.

Experience shows that you need to set aside two days or so to allow for last minute meetings to be arranged.

You should have completed your main objectives during your two weeks of intensive visits and discussions and hopefully come away feeling that you have chosen the best market for your products. You may, of course, repeat this exercise in other cities or territories before finally returning home.

2. Choice of exhibition

The next step after identifying and selecting the potential market you want to aim at is to choose the right exhibition(s) to enable you to reach your audience effectively. You normally have a choice of not only local and national but also international exhibitions. In many cases — and especially if your sales are primarily within one industry or service and of little interest to others — you will almost certainly want to have a stand at the one or two well-known and established exhibitions which are clearly market leaders in their field. If, on the other hand, your products or services extend across a wide range of sectors your choice will be much harder. You should set yourself a number of marketing objectives which can in turn serve as guidelines for choosing or rejecting one or more possible exhibitions.

Be wary of coming to a decision too quickly: the choice of exhibition should neither be based on the persuasive powers of exhibition organisers nor on the glowing success or failure stories you may hear or read about in the trade press. Remember that judgements about exhibitions tend to be very subjective. Whilst the views of others are, of course, always to be welcomed and taken into account, do not forget that their products, services and motives for taking part in exhibitions are almost bound to differ from your own objectives despite the apparent similarities in products or services being offered. Established businesses in a given field seldom share the same reasons for exhibiting as do the new and expanding companies. Think through carefully why YOU feel you should take space and select the appropriate exhibition which YOU feel most closely meets all YOUR marketing objectives. It is no good considering taking a stand just because other companies do! An analysis of who is and who is not represented at exhibitions quickly reveals that there is nearly always a number of well-known organisations who have decided not to have a stand. Are they the wise or foolish ones?

BASIC QUESTIONS

1. Ask the exhibition organisers for all the written material they can supply for their forthcoming exhibition. The material you receive may include:

A map of the exhibition centre
Registration regulations and forms
A leaflet outlining the services provided by the exhibition organisers
Details of special events

Evaluate the literature and ask yourself whether it is professionally and attractively produced.

If you need information on what exhibitions are planned check with: Data Book for Exhibitions, Trade Fairs & Conference Centres UK and Europe (ISBN 0 610 00594 4) published by: Information Services Ltd, Windsor Court, East Grinstead House, East Grinstead, West Sussex RH19 1XB Tel: 0342 26972. In the case of the U.S. obtain a copy of 'Annual Exhibitions and Fair Book'.

2. Try to obtain a copy of last year's catalogue. Is it well-produced and prestigious? This will show you who exhibited previously. Are the names familiar? Are your competitors listed? Who is missing?

3. Request a list of visitors to last year's exhibition. Many exhibition organisers compile lists of visitors broken down by name, job title, profession, trade, country of origin, etc. It is usually worth focusing on the job titles and especially if you want to appeal to a broad market. Ask yourself whether the job titles of those who attended last year are appropriate to you. Do buyers, specifiers, managers and decision makers feature strongly? Do they work for the kind of companies who use or may use your products, etc.? Are they attached to the 'right' kind of organisations? In some cases breakdowns of visitors' interests are also available by products or services and by the interest shown in particular parts of the exhibition. Does this kind of information indicate that you are likely to meet the kind of potential customers you wish to attract? Detailed computer print-outs of visitors are often available, and may be able to tell you a lot more about the visitors, their trade or profession, size of business, etc. If this data is available it can help you to decide whether the proposed exhibition really is appropriate to your requirements.

4. Request marketing data from the exhibition organisers. The kind of data available varies widely but some will be glad to furnish useful information which was collected from previous exhibitions, eg. the interest shown by visitors in specific sections of the show, the value of orders placed for different products or categories, the number of visitors at different times and days and the average time spent at the exhibition and the reasons they gave for coming to the exhibition, etc.

5. Find out what profession or trade organisations may be supporting or sponsoring the exhibition. Establish the names of members in such organisations and classify them according to YOUR interests, and the products or services YOU wish to promote.

6. Find out how the exhibition organisers will be promoting the event. Are the plans sufficiently ambitious and

imaginative to attract the 'right' number and quality of visitors? Will the exhibition be attracting the kind of PR coverage you require in the specialist press and other media?

7. Find out from the appropriate trade body whether a special collective or co-operative exhibition stand is perhaps being considered or organised which may suit your company.

8. Check whether any other firms known to you have exhibited there in the past: ask them for their opinions and experiences. Find out what trade and professional bodies may feel about the exhibition: are they supportive or critical?

9. If possible try to talk to some of those who had a stand at a previous exhibition — can they provide any interesting comments or pointers?

10. When considering a really major exhibition it is a good idea to try to visit the exhibition as an observer first. You can then verify for yourself all the information you have gleaned from others and make your own judgements before committing yourself to taking space at the next exhibition. For example:

- Look at competing products and services and how they are being exhibited.

- Check on the quality of associated and back-up services offered by the exhibition organiser e.g. are there meeting rooms, banking or photocopying facilities, etc.

- Check the actual flow of visitors. For this purpose, you should visit the exhibition on several occasions at different times of the day. Try also to evaluate daily 'special events' and promotions: could any of these provide opportunities for you?

- Check on the physical location of the spaces which you might like to take (or have been offered).

BEFORE REACHING A DECISION

Don't be hasty in coming to a decision about booking space at a specific exhibition before you have asked yourself such questions as:

a. Is the exhibition really suitable for your organisation and your products? Wander around the exhibition to gain a general impression. It is best to choose what you regard as the most interesting stand, and start your tour there. Visit a variety of stands which interest you with a view of collecting together your impressions. You can also stop at stands — where there are not too many visitors — and ask the exhibitors on the spot about the flow of visitors and what they feel about the level of inquiries or sales, etc.

b. Where is the flow of visitors strongest?

c. Where are the more interesting exhibitors' stands situated?

d. Where do you feel your stand should be? What are your second and third choices?

e. What space do the exhibition organisers want to offer you? At many exhibitions certain locations are earmarked for established exhibitors or for those reserving a stand well in advance. You may get special preference as a first-time exhibitor, but remember that often organisers allocate stands to those booking quickly and paying promptly.

f. Make a point of meeting the exhibition organisers. Ask for an option on the stand(s) you find most suitable. Ask about terms of payment. Check with contractors and suppliers of services and find out about the charges and deadlines.

g. It is a worthwhile exercise to fill in a simple questionnaire for every exhibition you may be considering as per the following example. Many of the details can be filled in before going along to an exhibition: the rest should be readily available from the literature, the exhibition organisers or your own records.

QUESTIONNAIRE FOR EXHIBITIONS AND FAIRS

Name of exhibition:

Location:

Dates: Days: Hours:

Total exhibition area (sq. mtrs):

Number of exhibition halls and floors:

Type of exhibition (Professional, National, International, General, Trade, Local):

Name and address of Exhibition Organisers:

Name & Tel. No. of contact:

Availability of previous exhibition data:

Total number of visitors:

Percentage analysis of main kinds of visitors eg:

1. Importers-Wholesalers:

2. Professional:

3. Distributors:

4. Institutional Buyers:

5. Representatives:

6. Other:

Total number of exhibitors (check the Exhibition Catalogue):

By main countries of origin:

The status and importance of the exhibition:

Other background information:

Sales achieved during the last exhibition according to the organisers eg:

Group A   Sales £
Group B   Sales £
Group C   Sales £

List YOUR key aims for participating at the exhibition eg:

1. Locating agents and distributors
2. Locating importers
3. General Sales promotion
4. Studying competitors (prices, products, packaging, etc.)
5. Co-operation in research, production, marketing
6. Study of market conditions (financing, agents' commission, etc)
7. Locating new products and technologies
8. Other (specify):

Recommendations for participation:

1. Leading manufacturers:
2. Government departments:
3. Commercial attaches:
4. Chamber of Commerce:
5. Professional organisations:
6. Other:

3. The Best Location

Choosing the best location for your stand is a tricky business. To start with you are seldom in a position to choose your ideal site: it may already be firmly booked, reserved or simply too expensive!

In coming to a sensible decision about location get hold of a detailed plan of the exhibition hall showing the stand layout and pay careful attention to the following:

1. Where are the entrances and exits?

2. Can you be located in any area opposite or close to the entrance so that all visitors will see and pass your stand first?

3. Generally speaking the public tend to turn right when they come into an exhibition hall. This area is therefore preferable to the space on the left of the entrance. Remember also that any visitors who may cut short their visit and leave via one of the main gangways are most likely to have seen your stand if it is on the right hand side.

4. Try not to be located at the far end (or top floor) of an exhibition hall even if you are offered preferential or reduced rates! If the exhibition hall is a large one, ask yourself whether visitors are likely to find you. Will all existing as well as potential customers reach a stand in the furthest corners of the hall or will they make it to(say) a stand on the second floor?

5. Try to select a stand bordering on one of the main gangways. Usually most visitors pass along these main routes and return by them as well: there is therefore a good chance that they will notice your stand both on their way in and when they leave the hall. Should they have missed you first time round there is at least a fair chance that they will spot you on their return trip.

6. Generally speaking try to avoid locating yourself in a side gangway or on an upper floor unless you have good reasons for choosing such locations. Of course, the venue, layout and size of an exhibition may be such that that you have to make compromises. There may also be special circumstances which dictate that you do locate in a particular area or floor already allocated to a particular type or size of business.

7. If there is a heavy demand for space be wary of exhibition organisers who attempt to offer you marginal areas such as corners or corridors which would normally be left empty. Where space is at a premium and demand is high some organisers may also attempt to persuade you to take space which is outside of the main exhibition area itself. Be very wary of such locations as they are unlikely to attract the same number of visitors as the main exhibition centre itself and seldom offer good value for money!

8. Normally a stand located at the end of a row of stands and open on two or more sides is preferable to a stand in the middle of the row and closed on three sides.

9. Try to choose a location close to refreshment, buffet, toilet, telephone or rest room facilities. These areas are usually full of people and you are likely to attract more attention.

10. As a general rule try to locate yourself close to areas where things are happening such as special events, celebrity appearances, information desks, demonstration areas, etc.

CHECKING OUT THE EXHIBITION LAYOUT

Have a good look at the plans for the exhibition. Take, for example, the McCormick Place Exhibition Centre in Chicago, USA, outlined in Figure 1, which illustrates the variety of stands, usually available at most exhibitions.

1. Island Areas: The ones marked (1) have four completely open sides so that visitors can inspect the stand on all four sides. Space such as this is normally considered to be the best as far as exposure is concerned. Of the two Island Stands 1304, for example, is a better proposition than 1516. It is not only larger but closer to the entrance, main gangways and the International Business Centre (Stand 200).
Island Sites provide the designer with plenty of scope for developing an exciting layout. However, the cost and associated expenses of taking such premium space is high especially if the space involves using non-standard fixtures and fittings.

2. Peninsular Areas: Stands (2) all have three open sides so that visitors can walk around them. Clearly there is a difference between stands 904 and 804. Whilst the first has a wide front facing the entrance, the second has two long fronts (55 ft.) which give maximum exposure along two gangways. The designer will have to use very different approaches in planning either stand and may well have to adapt fixtures and fittings including displays, signs, etc., to make the best impact within the space available.

3. 'L' Shaped Areas: Stands (3) are located in the corners of the hall. Their advantage is that they offer two fronts onto the gangway. Here too there are preferences: stands 1900 and 1901 are preferable to 100 and 200 because the former are on the right hand side and have wider openings.

4. Corner Areas: Stands such as (4) also offer two fronts but they are normally situated at the end of a block of stands and are therefore seen first by visitors. Note the dif-

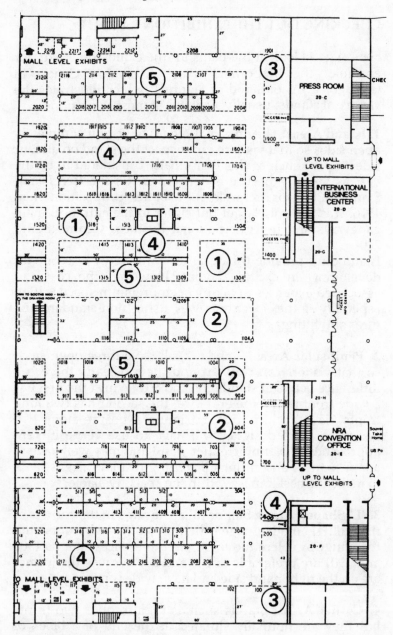

Figure 1. Example of Exhibition Layout

ference between stands 400, 217 and 1814 in terms of location, size and rental costs.

5. Standard Areas: These (5) types of stand are suitable for small exhibitors: they all have only one front and the exhibits and visuals can only be seen from one direction. Standard accessories, partitions, lighting, shelving, desks, etc., will normally fit such stands and can be hired from the contractors if booked well in advance — compare, for example, the pros and cons of stands 2108, 1313 and 1013.

4. The Right Design

A number of basic ground rules will help you to design an effective stand:

a. Stands should be functional

You should be aiming for a stand which not only provides adequate space for exhibiting your products or services but also gives ready access to visitors, comfortable seating for exhibitors and guests and some storage facilities which are hidden from general view. Remember that you are trying to sell your products or services and not the stand itself!

However attractive your stand may be, do not forget that its prime function is to attract the greatest number of potential buyers to see what you are offering and to sit down with you to discuss business. Therefore your prime concern should be to design a stand which is functionally effective: do not be side-tracked by a designer's vivid imagination (usually accompanied by costly plans). Be original and 'different' by all means, but do not detract from a stand which really meets all your basic requirements.

b. Design within the limits of the space available

Example 1: An area (of say) 15 square metres (5 m. wide by 3 m. deep and 2.82 m. high) is not the kind of stand which offers extensive scope for elaborate design. By the time you have used the back and side walls for displaying pro-

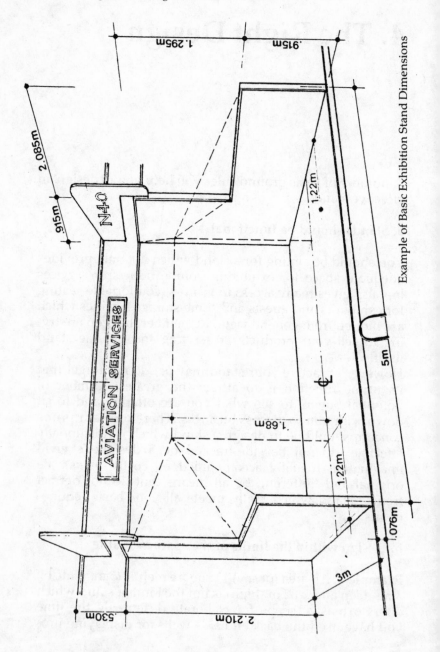

Example of Basic Exhibition Stand Dimensions

ducts or visuals, installed a table for exhibiting your product at the front and a small additional table with chairs for you and your guests, your stand will already be full!

Example 2: A smaller stand (of say) 10 square metres (5 m. long by 2m. deep) offers even less scope for innovative designs. Be careful not to try to do too much within such relatively small spaces.

c. Keep the design simple and attractive

The designer can achieve much by combining colour, graphics, photos and lighting. Key product exhibits should be displayed allowing adequate space between each. Show one sample of important products but keep extra samples out of view under the table allowing easy retrieval should they be required.

d. Choose a central product or exhibit

Ideally select one product or theme. This should attract attention and help to direct visitors to your other exhibits. By all means exploit walls and partitions for drawings, graphics and pictures, but where feasible — and especially when space is limited — try to focus attention on one key product or service.

There is nothing worse than a stand which presents the visitor with just too many messages especially within the confines of a small stand. Remember that your stand is only one of many (often hundreds) of others. Your stand has to compete with all the others for attention. Most of us can only take in a very limited amount of information and images at any one time. We are quickly side-tracked and lose interest if you don't easily get a clear sales message across. Whatever else your stand may try to do, it should be conveying quickly and simply what your business or service are all about. You have to try to design a stand which at least causes the passerby to pause and stop and, hopefully, find an excuse to come and talk to you about what you have to offer. In a nutshell, you have just a few seconds in which you can make an initial impact!

e. Larger Stands

In the case of larger stands — especially national stands where the public can wander around one large prestigious stand — pay special attention to planning the movement of people. Erecting an office for private meetings and special storage facilities plus providing sufficient seating for all exhibitors and visitors is usually essential for such stands.

f. Separate Pavilions

In special cases it may be necessary to put up a separate exhibition pavilion within or outside the exhibition hall. This involves high costs and a great deal of planning including the services of designers and architects as well as specialist contractors to erect, maintain and finally dismantle the structure. Figure 2, for example, shows the Israeli pavilion at the 'Salon de l'Aviation' in Paris.

g. Financial Control

Budgets are essential for all exhibition stands. You may get by with 'ball park' figures for the really small stand, but it is all too easy for costs to get out of hand unless basic budgetary constraints are imposed. Without proper financial control and budgetary disciplines the designer tends to propose costly solutions. Try to pre-plan for all items of expenditure and make sure you have a budget provision before incurring further ad-hoc costs.

5. Exhibiting your Products

It is worth stressing that potential customers are primarily interested in seeing your actual products for themselves. Photos, drawings, models and diagrams may all have a part to play in making an attractive and interesting stand but they are never a substitute for the real thing! Avoid any temptation to exhibit unfinished samples or prototypes: your potential customers want to see your finished products which are in stock and available for delivery now!

Not only do customers want to see products for themselves; they also want to see them working. They want to touch and examine them and check out whether they meet their specific needs.

Therefore if you are exhibiting:

a. machinery, make sure it is in working order,

b. an instrument, demonstrate how it actually works,

c. fresh or processed food, let the public taste it for themselves,

d. fashion goods, arange for models to show your clothes or accessories off to their best advantage.

Whatever the product, you must try to appeal to as many senses as possible. They will all help to attract customers' attention, interest and curiosity and lead to requests for further information. From here on success depends on you!

CHECKING YOUR STAND

The following checklist will help you to check all the products on your stand:

1. Personally ensure that all products chosen for the exhibition are in perfect condition, i.e. not scratched, corroded, damaged or faulty.

2. Ensure that the complete product or machine and any key accessories are available: there should be no missing parts.

3. It is important that the product exhibited should match the description given in the brochures you are distributing to potential customers.

4. Do not apologise to customers with remarks such as 'this is only a sample . . .' or 'the final product we are selling will be far superior to the one shown here . . .
Remember customers want to see the actual finished (and working) product. If you start making excuses they will immediately turn to the nearest competitor.

5. Ensure that brochures or leaflets which come with the product or machinery are not all 'sales talk' but contain hard facts about performance levels, operating instructions, maintenance, etc.

6. Check that all references in the literature (and on packing labels) include units of measurement which are appropriate to specific market(s) you are aiming at (kgs, litres, etc.).

7. In the case of electrical equipment check carefully that the voltage, leads, plugs and safety regulations etc. are right for the market and customers you are trying to attract.

8. If the machinery on display is in working order, take out appropriate insurance cover to safeguard against accidental injury to third parties.

9. Remember that exhibits should ideally be so arranged that they are all clearly visible by those passing your stand: avoid 'hiding' exhibits in corners. A great deal of space is required just to allow the public easy access to your stand and any displays or working machines you may have. In the case of consumer goods you may need to allow as much as a third of the space on your stand for this purpose: when exhibiting industrial products you may need to allow as much as 60 per cent of the total space available especially if your products are machines or major items of equipment.

10. It is important to plan for the optimum height at which exhibits can be seen by everybody. That means that even if your stand is busy and has many visitors, all key exhibits should remain visible and not be obscured by the visitors.

11. Make sure you have an ample reserve stock of samples (especially at consumer goods exhibitions) so that you can replenish samples given away or replace any damaged stock. It is also common for odd items to 'disappear' or be removed from a stand and you should be prepared to have replacements readily available to fill any gaps.

12. Ensure that you have some spotlights as well as general background lighting. The lighting should always be directed onto products and exhibits and never the public. For example, in glass counters displaying jewellery, ensure that lighting does not shine in customers' faces but on the products in the showcase.

SHELL STANDS

Basic Shell Stands consist of walls, fascia and mid supports and ceiling beams, with signwritten stand number and name sign (1 per open side). The entire exhibition area is close covered in brown Heugafelt carpet tiles.

IMPORTANT - STAND WALLS

Panels and fascia are beige loop nylon covered, and the main structure is of polished anodised aluminium, consisting of an eight sided upright, with rectangular horizontal beams between. Basic module is 990 mm centres (1 metre nominal) and multiples thereof. Intermediate fascia support posts are at intervals not exceeding 4 metres. Larger stands may have internal support posts as detailed on individual stand layout. A diagonal ceiling grid of beams is provided, save where stands are 3 metres or less in depth, when corner bracing is fitted instead of wall/fascia junctions. Internal clearance height of shell scheme - 2.7m.

Fixings of heavy items are not permitted direct to the stand wall panels, but a complete range of fixings is available to fit to the aluminium sections. Velcro pads are available to attach light exhibits to the loop nylon walls. **Please do not use double sided pads or pins for fixing - both damage the panels and you will be charged for their repair/replacement.**

Example of Organiser's Exhibition Stand Specifications

13. Check that you have a prominent signboard with your name (in the country's language) at the front of the stand.

14. Every sign should be clear, short and to the point. No potential buyers will take the trouble to approach your stand in order to read a long story in small sized print. Make sure that any text you do use is concise and in a large enough typesize to be read from a reasonable distance. Put yourself in the visitors' shoes and take a critical look at your own graphics and displays. Ask yourself whether you readily get a clear message or is the overall impression 'messy'? Is it clear what your business is? Is it clear what products you are promoting?

15. All descriptions of products or services must clearly be in the local language.

16. Avoid handwritten signs — they are usually difficult to read. Stick to bold lettering and large typesizes and remember that any photographs and displayed text needs to be sufficiently enlarged for easy reading.

17. It is important to add a sales message to all technical product data. By all means provide detailed technical specifications but also give the potential customer some ideas of your product's benefits, practical applications, unusual characteristics, etc.

18. In appropriate circumstances weigh up the pros and cons of showing a short video, using an electronic message board or giving a brief slide presentation: all can help to attract people to your stand.

19. In all but the smallest stands try to arrange for an area to be set aside (an office or screened area is best) where you can sit quietly and comfortably with a customer without being disturbed. Allow perhaps two extra chairs for waiting customers. Although space limitations may make this difficult to achieve, don't forget that exhibition stand

designers and planners tend to want to give the whole area over to displays and exhibits. Your job is to see to it that you and your customers have space for meetings and sales negotiations!

20. Keep a constant watch over your catalogues and brochures — don't let them lie about amongst the exhibits and end up being knocked on the floor. Use proper leaflet dispensers or hand them out to interested visitors.

21. Exhibition handbooks or manuals tend not to be carefully read. However, make sure you know where to go for what services. Use the exhibition organiser's forms for ordering lighting, booking advertising space, catalogue entries, etc., and make sure you keep to the deadlines indicated.

22. If you have a small stand within the framework of a larger national stand or pavilion, make sure you keep in close touch with the organisers so that all your efforts are co-ordinated. Are you clear about who is responsible for what?

6. Finding potential buyers

Most exhibitions attract large numbers of visitors and at peak times you and your colleagues are likely to come under considerable pressure. It is especially important at these times to be able to identify and classify visitors quickly in your mind so that you can offer each one the attention they deserve. Remember that most exhibitions, including the highly specialised ones, attract a wide variety of visitors and only some are likely to be potential customers. You should be focusing your attention on this group, but unless you can readily spot these people you are in danger of wasting a great deal of time. Generally speaking you can classify visitors into three broad categories:

1. Those who may be curious or show an interest but are not potential customers.

2. Those who show a genuine interest: some may be potential customers in the future.

3. Those showing a keen interest in your products or services now and are definitely prospective customers.

The nuisance visitor

1. THE FIRST CATEGORY INCLUDE:

a. 'The nuisance visitor'

These are the people who come up to your stand simply to put their feet up, engage in casual conversation or avail themselves (hopefully) of any free refreshments there may be. Try to avoid wasting time with these characters: if you make them welcome they are liable to make themselves at home on your stand for a long time! Often the solution is to find a polite yet firm excuse. Say something like 'I expect to have an urgent meeting shortly' or 'Can we set up a meeting in an hour's time' (hopefully this will deter the nuisance visitor and you won't see that person again!). Alternatively try asking 'which product are you interested in?' or see whether 'Can I assist you in some way' will deter them.

b. 'The inquisitive visitor'

Such people are really a sub-species of the 'nuisance visitor'. They are not interested in any of your products or services but stop by in order to kill time. They typically ask general questions and are also often avid collectors of all leaflets within reach! You will have to find ways of dealing with such visitors. One approach which usually works is to ask them 'which company do you represent' or 'what line of business are you in?'. Hopefully you will be given an answer or lead which enables you to terminate the conversation quickly.

c. 'The old friend'

We all know about the old friends or acquaintances who just happen to drop in on your stand: they are usually not interested in doing business. They either know you or somebody in your organisation or are sending you greetings from someone you mutually know. They may want to discuss the 'good old times', the economic or political situ-

The inquisitive visitor

ation, the weather or just have a cosy chat about their recent holiday. Whatever the reason they can take up a great deal of your time chatting away amicably. You must remember that this is not why you are at the exhibition. If they really are good friends and you want to meet them try to arrange a social meeting one evening after the exhibition is closed.

d. 'The general public'

Of course, if you are dealing with consumer goods you are most likely to welcome the general public to your stand. However, in trade or specialist exhibitions you are usually trying to appeal to business people or professionals. A number of exhibitions these days attempt to appeal both to the trade and the public at large by setting aside certain days (or times of the day) when the general public are admitted. Often name badges are colour coded to enable you to readily distinguish the various categories of visitor.

The pros and cons of such arrangements clearly depend very much on the kind of products or services you are offering. However, be wary of distributing expensive catalogues and leaflets to all and sundry. There may indeed be a number of genuine and interesting enquiries from non-trade sources, but you certainly need to guard against the keen 'catalogue collectors' who pick up vast copies of all glossy literature within reach. Much of this is discarded on the way out and some exhibition organisers even go so far as to provide waste bins just for this purpose!

Remember, too, that there is a strong case for being security conscious of your stand and your exhibits especially when the general public is admitted. Talk to any regular exhibitor or exhibition organiser and you will find that they all have stories to tell about 'disappearing' exhibits. Although the majority of pilfering is of a minor kind, it is certainly not unknown for quite large pieces of equipment or machinery to disappear when your back is turned. Be especially vigilant when there are lots of people around your stand.

2. SECONDLY, THE 'INTERESTED NON-CUSTOMERS'

This group includes those visitors who show some interest in your products but are unlikely to be customers in the near future. Also in this category are journalists who are looking for stories about new products, and VIPs and students, etc.

a. Journalists

They are mainly interested in new products and stories about product successes and failures. If you have an unusual stand or are staging demonstrations, for example, you may also provide the background for a newsworthy story. Inquisitive journalists may sometimes take up a lot of your time but it is usually worthwhile. Remember that journalists are busy people and it will, therefore, normally be sensible to have attractive press folders containing news, leaflets and photographs available: always give the name, address and telephone number of someone from whom further information can be obtained.

Not only do press folders save your time, but they also ensure that journalists take with them the sales and technical information YOU want them to have. Whether you will subsequently necessarily like the piece they write about your products is another matter. Hopefully what you read will at least be based in part on data included in the press folder. It should also mean that errors are kept to a minimum.

Journalists from the specialist or trade press should be made particularly welcome for that they write will be read

Nearly all exhibitions attract some VIP visitors.....

by an important market segment. Most journalists working for the technical press have plenty of experience and background knowledge. Therefore be prepared for more searching questions and, if appropriate, have further detailed literature available for them. Remember that good editorial coverage is very valuable promotion for your activities and costs you absolutely nothing! The same amount of space in the advertising columns would cost you a great deal of money and may not be so effective.

b. VIPs

These days nearly all exhibitions attract some VIP guests and visitors. They range from government ministers, members of parliament, mayors, local and governmental officials to ambassadors, attaches and directors of public institutions, etc. Usually the exhibition organisers notify exhibitors of key VIP visits, but if they do come along without prior warning they can usually be easily recognised by their large entourage and their identification tags.

Whilst few VIPs are likely to be prospective customers, they demand full attention and a warm welcome. Be prepared to talk about all kinds of topics which have little or nothing to do with your specific stand or products! Be prepared for photographers and if a VIP does stop at your stand, seize the opportunity to take your own photographs: they can be useful for newsletters and future brochures.

c. Students

Generally speaking students are likely to be interested in new products and technology. They can easily take up a lot of your time, but remember that some may become your customers in future years. How much time you give them depends on the pressures you are under at your stand and what value you attach to longer term goodwill and PR. If you have made prior arrangements for an organised group visit, ensure that you are available and make your presentation succinct and interesting bearing in mind the age and interests of the students. Keep a tight control on your literature when students are around!

3. THIRDLY, THE 'REAL CUSTOMERS'

The third and final broad category of visitors — the 'professionals' and trade customers — are the group you are really trying to attract to your stand. Experience shows that this, too, is a very diverse group: you will soon acquire considerable expertise in spotting the various types of visitors and develop an ability to recognise the most likely prospects.

Can you, for example, pick out those visitors who are really interested in your products or services by:

- their appearance?
- their visitor's name tag?
- their accent or language?
- the interest shown in your literature?
- the time spent on your stand?
- the kind of questions asked?

Some or all of these factors (and, of course, others) may help you to weigh up the different visitors you have, but it is helpful to go into a little more detail and try to group your prospective customers into the following categories:

a. 'The purchasing initiator'

These may include scientists, researchers, laboratory staff, engineers, designers, architects, etc. All these kind of people are likely to be interested in your products, initiate further enquiries and recommend purchase. Be prepared to answer a broad range of detailed questions on, for example:

- technical matters
- quality standards
- material specifications
- maintenance
- your literature
- names of other users, etc.

Remember that this group of visitors will expect you to demonstrate a high level of professional and technical know-how in answering their queries. However, if you build up a rapport with such visitors you will find that most will readily share their know-how and experiences with you. They are also usually only too willing to refer you to other useful colleagues and contacts.

b. Those with influence

They also tend to come with a diverse range of job titles — it may be the person in charge of purchasing at a public institution (such as a hospital), the buyer from a private company or the purchasing manager of a large industrial plant. Whatever their job title may be all of these visitors will show an interest in prices, terms of payments, discounts, etc., but they generally disclose very little else.

You should have well-prepared commercial information readily available to answer the kind of questions they are likely to ask. How do your prices compare with the competitors? What credit facilities are available? What are your terms of business? etc.

Consider whether it may be sensible to try and meet your visitor again after the exhibition. You may need to spend more time finding out precisely what he requires and how the machinery, for example, fits in with other existing plant and processes. Another meeting can also help to build up confidence and perhaps produce a firm order.

However, before arranging another meeting weigh up

very carefully whether it is likely to be productive. Remember that generally speaking European buyers are prepared to devote, say, one hour of their time to you. The Japanese buyer on the other hand may give you two days and the Americans only ten minutes. Judge what is appropriate in each specific case: make a point of being strictly factual and concise with the Americans and tolerant as well as interesting when negotiating with the Japanese!

c. 'The end user'

These may be the operators or perhaps in some cases the managers, supervisors and professionals, etc., who actually want the product. They have plenty of practical experience and usually know all about raw materials, processes of production, etc. They are, in the main, professionals who, if approached properly, are prepared to talk freely about their achievements and failures. If you manage to arouse their curiosity and encourage them to compare the advantages and drawbacks of materials and products, there is a good chance that they will go on to discuss the methods and processes used in their plant quite openly. It is important to gain the goodwill and interest of this group of visitors since their views may well determine the final decision about purchasing. If you are, for example, selling printers' inks, it is the machine operator or foreman who is likely to decide whether to use your inks or not.

d. 'The decision maker'

Again this group comes in all guises: it may be the owner of a business, the plant manager, the project manager and many others. He may come to your stand accompanied by a professional adviser, a sales manager or a financial expert.

These visitors will usually show an interest in the overall advantages of the product, details of ordering and delivery, servicing, maintenance, storage and promotion. Even though they generally make prior appointments they are likely to show up at your stand unexpectedly.

e. 'The buyer with the purse strings'

Sometimes the owner of a business, company chairman, managing director or finance director may turn up at your stand. However senior they may be, remember that even top management has to (or should have to) work within budgetary controls or obtain the consent of the head of finance (or whatever he may be called)!

The irony is that though you may have been successful in your negotiations with the person you thought was a decision maker when he called at your stand, you may not have been talking to the man with the budgetary authority to purchase. Very often the person with the budgetary responsibility does not go to exhibitions at all. Many promising sales leads may get 'stuck', linger on indefinitely or simply just 'die'. The moral is to try to establish who really holds the purse strings! It is certainly not uncommon for the keen prospective customer to find that on return to his organisation he is overruled by colleagues for a variety of reasons.

SUMMARY

Understanding and distinguishing between the different kinds of visitors who call at your stand is most important. Remember that sometimes two or more of the characteristics we have outlined may be found in one person. The owner of a small business may not only be the initiator, but also the end-user, the decision maker and the controller of finance all rolled into one!

As a general rule the larger the company, the more complex the purchasing process is. It is also usually the case that the more expensive the prospective purchase, the more people will be involved in the buying decision. In the case of major products you should therefore make a point of trying to identify and influence them all. Since it is unlikely that all of them will come to the exhibition you may have to arrange a visit to the customer after the exhibition is over.

It is important for you to find out what you can about a company's purchasing policies and practices: try also to establish who is involved in the purchasing decision-making process and ask yourself whether there is anything you can do to achieve a favourable outcome.

OTHER KINDS OF VISITORS

Visitors to your stand will not all be prospective customers, journalists, VIPs, etc. Be prepared to deal with a range of other visitors, some of whom will be interested in representing your company in other countries or perhaps selling you something.

a. The prospective agent

At many exhibitions you will be visited by people offering to represent you or act as an agent in the country where the exhibition is being held or elsewhere.

The key piece of advice in such circumstances is not to sign any agreements on the spot: you must give such offers careful consideration and visit the people concerned in their offices so that their facilities, etc., can be properly evaluated.

If you are actively interested in finding new agents or distributors consider displaying a sign 'AGENTS WANTED'. The exhibition organisers should also be informed as they usually provide a service to put exhibitors and prospective agents in touch with each other.

On the other hand if you already have representatives or agents covering certain countries or market segments and do not want to be pestered with calls from would be agents say so. Display a simple sign saying 'Our agent(s) in . . . is (are) . . .' This will avoid time wasting for everybody!

b. Salesmen

Whether you like it or not some callers at your stand are likely to offer to sell you something. It may be raw materials, equipment or a wide range of services in the legal, technical, financial and marketing fields. Be patient! You may not have come to the exhibition to be sold products or services but you never know what possible opportunities may arise in such cases. You may find a suitable product to import or a worthwhile service you are just looking for. Take any relevant leaflets offered and get full details of prices, delivery, etc. if it looks interesting. Try to keep such meetings brief and friendly.

c. Other visitors interested in collaboration or investment

Again there are a wide variety of possibilities. Some people may be interested in your products and want to manufacture them locally: they will need know-how, special tools and equipment which you can perhaps provide. Others may be interested in adding your product to their existing range and so broaden their marketing base. You may also have a visit from a financier who is looking for investment opportunities and may suggest ways he might finance the further development of your products.

It should be a rule in all these and similar cases that you do not come to any decisions there and then. Such proposals demand thorough investigation and above all satisfactory answers to many questions. You will also need to examine and check various facts and figures before you can come to a decision on whether and how to proceed.

It sometimes happens that you feel under pressure in such situations especially if the closing date for the exhibition is approaching and you feel you have to return to base with tangible results.

Exercise caution if a person suddenly appears on your stand on the last day with an offer of collaboration or investment in some way. Emotionally you may be prepared to grasp the opportunity and sign an agreement on the spot or in the time remaining till the exhibition closes. Restrain yourself from any rash thoughts of signing something: you need time to think matters through! By all means have further talks about the proposals in the evening back at the hotel and perhaps visit the enquirer's office for further discussions. However, there is a lot more to be done before you should be thinking of signing any formal agreement.

You have clearly to check the legal, financial, costing and other issues. Above all you must find out a lot more about your potential partner. Are you likely to be able to develop a long-term mutually satisfactory relationship? Have you considered the cultural differences, especially in the case of export business? Never ever entertain some kind of arrangement of this kind without spending a lot of time thinking carefully about all the issues and making sure you really do know enough about the other party involved.

It is difficult to set down any rules in this field. It is partly a matter of temperament and personality and sound business judgment. There are those who hasten to sign "while the iron is hot" and are successful. There are others who conduct thorough, long and time-consuming checks and yet still fail. Remember that both parties will be gathering

The professional industrial spy

information about each other. If you are aiming at some form of longer-term collaboration — as opposed to a single transaction — you both need to do your homework thoroughly before signing any agreement.

d. The professional industrial spy

Be wary of those who come to visit your stand several times and show considerable interest in the construction of your product and associated production methods, etc. They are likely to take a keen and close interest, make detailed notes of every aspect, ask for technical literature and perhaps even seek permission to take photographs in a static or operating mode!

These characters may even go as far as suggesting having some of your equipment on a trial basis with the sole intention of exploiting and copying your products.

Usually the industrial spy will have a carefully prepared cover story which you must try to crack as soon as possible. Start by asking detailed questions about identity. Ask for business cards and enquire into the size of company which he represents. Ask questions about other organisations with which you are familiar in his country. Find out what he or she knows about other people operating in your field. If you have asked the right questions about identity, the amateur spy will usually give up whilst the professional is usually able to withstand all your probing questions.

His persistence and your suspicions call for further questioning. Start with questions of quantity — how many items are required per year? How many similar products are sold in his country or area? From which country are they imported? What does he know about prices?

If all this does not flush out the professional spy, start talking about patents. For example, start by saying something like: 'We registered a patent for our product in your country and we don't wish to provide extra work for local lawyers . . .' Discourage his willingness to purchase a sample with the excuse that transport and other allied costs force you to sell in quantities of at least one full container load or for a minimum sum of money. If your product is complex, stress that professional 'after sales' service is required and that essential spares must be bought and held in stock, etc. Ask whether he can provide you with introductions to other customers.

If after all these and similar questions you receive satisfactory answers, you may indeed have found a real customer!

Remember that every visitor to your stand may be a potential spy, be they amateur or professional! However it is no good becoming obsessed with real or imaginery industrial spies. Do not get side tracked by such distractions but carry on your efforts to sell your products to 'real' customers — this will be the ultimate measure of your success.

e. The real purchaser

Your aim should always to be devote most of your time to existing or new customers. Buyers of consumer goods often place orders at exhibitions: they are usually in the nature of trial orders for new products. On the other hand buyers of industrial goods generally prefer to place orders after they have examined your products and found that they meet their requirements.

7. Guidelines for negotiations

Negotiating effectively requires experience and skills: helpful books covering the subject in detail are listed in the further reading section at the end of this volume. Suffice to say here that the most important traits when negotiating are: —

- patience
- creativity & inventiveness
- a relaxed manner
- self-confidence

At the conclusion of a successful negotiation both parties should be satisfied. They should also both accept that they have had to retreat from certain attitudes and agree to compromises. Negotiations can be tough and create tensions: ensure that once completed any unpleasantness which may have emerged in the course of your discussions is put firmly behind you. Remember you are both trying to develop a successful ongoing relationship. A quiet meal after everything is agreed is a good way to seal a deal and get over any heated discussions there may have been previously.

NEGOTIATING CHECKLIST

The following checklist highlights some of the key points you should bear in mind when negotiating: they have been proven over many years experience of conducting negotiations abroad:

1. Always enter negotiations with a clear idea of the results you wish to achieve. Where possible pre-plan compromise positions you are willing to accept.

2. Try to construct a scenario of the negotiations asking yourself a series of 'what if' type questions. Plan a few stages ahead and try to take into account all possible options.

3. If you are invited to a customer's offices, make sure beforehand that the people you are going to negotiate with are really the ones empowered to make decisions. Your time at exhibitions (especially overseas ones) is expensive: you cannot afford to waste time with 'middlemen' or the wrong people!

4. Open with a strong initial position in areas where you can permit yourself some leeway. Trade these, as appropriate, for concessions made by the other party: no wonder that negotiating is sometimes called 'trading compromises'.

5. Try to discover at an early stage in the discussion what the other side wishes to achieve. In particular try to establish what they want above all else.

6. If negotiations appear to get 'stuck' at a certain point try to settle other matters first and then return to the problematic issue at the end.

7. Never agree to make concessions only so that negotiations can continue. Stubbornness on an important issue is often more realistic than simply to continue the negotiations. Don't be afraid of slowing the discussions down so as to clarify a point.

8. Do not get worried if the other party threatens to discontinue negotiations. In most cases this is but a tactic to entice you to make further concessions. Be prepared for the 'last shot' just when it seems that everything has been settled. This is an old and well-known tactic in an attempt to extract last minute concessions from you.

9. Do not get involved in the negotiations emotionally as this is bound to cause failure!

10. Try not to negotiate on your own — a team of two or three colleagues is preferable and especially so if the deal is an important one.

11. Try to control the way the negotiations are conducted. Think of possible outcomes and leave yourself plenty of time for thought.

12. Questions play an important part in the negotiating process. Do not be afraid of asking them even if you may be considered frivolous or naive. It is much better to be absolutely clear about what is being discussed than sorry later!

13. Ignorance is not something to be ashamed of. Do ask any questions on topics that bother you and try to learn from the answers. Don't dominate the discussions: you must give your opposite number a chance to demonstrate his knowledge, skills and experience, etc.

14. Time is a key factor in the negotiating process. Businessmen tend to avoid wasting time and try to get directly to the point. Make sure your contributions are succinct and relevent.

15. Do not be afraid of making telephone calls or visits during negotiations — they can provide missing facts or figures and save time in the long run.

16. In order to give yourself time when dealing with a difficult point do not be afraid of exploiting breaks for meals, drinks and even visits to the cloakroom!

17. Food and drink are tools in the negotiating process. See to it that they act in your favour and are not allowed to distract or cloud your judgement.

18. Physical comfort is important when negotiating but do not be tempted to accept frequent invitations to meals or entertainment lest you develop a degree of dependence on your host's hospitality. Try to avoid talks that go on late into the night.

19. Remember that negotiations are not a competition with winners and losers. The outcome should satisfy both parties. Any agreement which puts the rights of one party at a severe disadvantage will not last long!

20. You must end up finalising a deal! Ensure that you summarise points of agreement and make sure that both parties are under no misunderstandings. Repeat the key points if there appear to be any doubts or ambiguities. Summarise the terms of payment and delivery and shipping details. Clarify the form the agreement will take — check this with your legal advisers.

21. Prepare a summary of all the points discussed during the negotiations with the other person's consent. Ideally you should try to finish a report of your meeting on the same day in your hotel room. Remember that memories are short and it is all too easy to forget important details even two days after a meeting. Make a point of sending your opposite number a written summary in the post.

8. On Your Best Behaviour

Courteous behaviour to people visiting your stand goes without saying — it reflects a good image of your organisation. Do not forget that your stand constitutes a shop window not just for your products but for the whole of your business as well.

Attractive and well-designed products are in themselves not enough. Your staff must know how to approach prospective customers, gain their interest and answer all their questions professionally. Hopefully they also know how to close a sale. They should also be at ease and good at developing informal personal relationships. The customer expects you not only to be courteous, punctual and patient but demonstrate that you have integrity and a good back-up organisation behind you.

Avoid:

- showing any impatience even under stressful conditions
- displaying exaggerated self-confidence (we can't know everything!)
- displaying your 'natural' superiority
- any tendency to behave aggressively
- being in any way discourteous
- untidy appearance.

Customers rightly expect impeccable behaviour when they visit your stand. They welcome a direct and open approach and a feeling of reliability and integrity. To hold attention you will need to improvise and handle potentially difficult situations sympathetically. You will also need to be able to demonstrate your organisation's past and present achievements in a convincing manner. These are all key ingredients if you are to be successful when making your initial contacts. If you wish to have an ongoing relationship and develop confidence over time, you will have to be able to deal effectively with the idiosyncrasies of your customers.

Be smart

- being smartly dressed in a suit — avoid ostentatious clothes
- wearing a sweater on cold days (if you have to and the stand is cold). Avoid overcoats, raincoats and scarves!
- wearing a clean white coat over your clothes if you are handling or demonstrating food, pharmaceutical or similar products
- bringing along a spare shirt on hot days so that you can change during the day and remain smart and fresh
- taking a towel and toilet gear with you. If you are then suddenly invited to a business meeting immediately after the exhibition closes and have no time to return to your hotel, you can have a wash and be ready for a meeting looking smart
- giving yourself enough time to wash, change and relax a little before attending evening appointments. It is bad policy to attempt to do too much — you need time to unwind after a long and busy day at the exhibition
- wearing light shoes on the stand. Remember you are walking on your feet all day and it is amazing how much standing and walking about you can do at an exhibition. In the evening and for social occasions you will want to use more formal footwear — check that your shoes are clean and polished at all times

- checking your personal appearance is important. Pack some spare handkerchiefs and tissues as they are always useful

Refreshments

- make sure your crockery and cutlery, etc., are spotlessly clean
- all snacks, biscuits, peanuts, etc., must be fresh. Make sure you have sufficient stocks
- clear away all glasses and dishes, etc., after each meeting. Obtain adequate supplies of disposable plates
- avoid eating on the stand! Do not greet a customer with a full mouth or greasy hands!
- do not smoke unless a visitor smokes first: have ashtrays available even if you do not smoke

On the Stand

- stay 'up front' — don't linger at the back of your stand and give the impression you do not want to see anybody!
- on the other hand do not give the impression you are guarding the stand by blocking all access!
- if you have colleagues with you do not all stand together as this will keep visitors away
- do not let your colleagues occupy all your seating — leave some free for visitors
- do not read a newspaper or look bored
- even though you may be tired, never greet customers sitting down

9. Expense Budget

Due to the level of expenditure involved in participating at exhibitions, especially overseas, you should plan and budget for costs beforehand. This is not only prudent but avoids the possibility of incurring heavy costs. Use the following checklist to help you prepare a budget.

BUDGET FOR EXHIBITION:

Date:

1. Registration fees (payable at some exhibitions abroad)

2. Rental expenses per square metre:

Check that discounts (if any) for specific locations or stand sizes have been given

3. Total cost of erecting the stand including the following alternatives:

a. Renting stand:
In the case of standard 'shells' find out what the rent covers (partitions, ceiling, fascia board, signs, lighting, etc.).

3. Designed stand:

If you are designing your own stand, the organisers often want to approve your plan before you proceed. You must ensure that you obtain prior approval where necessary and check that your dimensions, etc., are in keeping with the organiser's specifications. Check with the exhibition manual that you are complying with rules about permitted height of stands, fireproof paint for the walls, standard signs, etc.

Do not forget that expenses will include the designer's fee, preparing a model, graphic work, photographs, planning, erection of exhibits, decoration, lighting, etc. Remember that every change in your plan is likely to incur additional expense.

4. Doing it yourself:

Remember that at many exhibitions only a recognised contractor (and usually a sole contractor) is employed to handle all exhibitors' requirements.

You can save costs by preparing the plan and design of the stand 'in-house' and you may well have facilities for undertaking your own graphic work, signs and photographs. The actual erection of the stand is usually undertaken by a contractor under your supervision and direction.

5. A collective or national stand:

Normally the organising body will look after the planning and erection of the stand. You are responsible for having your goods ready for exhibition. Check with the co-ordinator what your responsibilities are if you are in any doubt.

6. Costs of electricity, gas and water:
Are these included in the stand price or extra? Check with the exhibitor's manual.

7. Cost of hiring furniture, etc.
This may include chairs, tables, shelves, coathangers, etc. Normally you can select any items required from the appointed contractor's catalogue: payment is usually in advance.

8. Carpeting:
At some exhibitions carpeting may be included in the price of the stand: at others you may have to acquire or hire it. Calculate whether or not it is worthwhile to buy and fit it and then use it again at subsequent exhibitions.

9. Costs for signwriting or graphic work:
Check whether signwriters (if required) are available on site: they are in some countries.

10. Costs for plants and flowers:
These are usually available on site or by prior booking from the organiser's contractors.

11. Telephone and communication costs:
This usually involves a connection charge (paid in advance) plus call costs (paid after the exhibition closes). You may also incur costs for telexes, facsimilies transmission, courier services, postage and parcels.

12. Stand clearing:
Check with the organisers who is responsible and whether the costs are included in the stand charge or not.

13. Miscellaneous items:
Dusters, waste bins, ashtrays, etc. If you do not bring them with you, buy some locally if you can.

14. Security costs:
Check details with the exhibition company.

15. Parking and visitors tickets:
Practice varies widely — sometimes exhibitors may have free car parking facilities and a small number of complimentary tickets for visitors. In other circumstances all parking and visitors tickets are chargeable (perhaps at advantageous rates).

16. Pay for 'exhibition only' staff:
This could include staff hired from agencies, casual local labour, translators and interpreters, secretarial help, etc. It is advisable to agree on an inclusive daily rate which covers pay, refreshments and travel expenses. Check with the organisers for details of the 'going' rates if you are not sure what to pay.

17. Insurance costs:
Check who is covering the risks of members of staff and locally employed labour. Are exhibition risks covered by any existing policies? Often third party insurance is covered by the exhibition organisers. Remember to cover exhibits and machinery, etc., whilst in transit and on show.

18. Entertaining budget:
It is often practical to buy items for your stand locally. Allow for disposable plates, cups and glasses.

19. Special Events budget:
These might include press conference costs, gifts, drinks parties and a photographer's fee.

20. Exhibition catalogue and poster costs:
Normally a catalogue entry for your organisation is free of charge (make sure you send off the details before the deadline and check the entry and proofs carefully). Advertising space in the catalogue and on poster sites within the exhibition may be worth considering. Check on the cost and decide. Add the cost of purchasing any additional catalogues you may require.

21. Cost of special exhibition leaflets or newsletters.

22. Advertising and PR costs.

23. Cost of transportation:
This might include costs of delivery and collecting exhibits and machinery, other carrier costs, porters, shipping agents, freight costs by sea or air, etc. Check whether the organisers have an approved transport contractor. Often you will have to use an exclusive agent: they may be expensive but you have no alternative course of action.

24. Miscellaneous (unexpected) expenses.

25. Finally, you may want to add (especially in the case of small companies) costs you have had to incur as a result of your absence from the office (eg. temporary staff.)

TOTAL EXPENDITURE

10. Running the Stand

Give prior attention to all the small details which are involved in setting up and running your stand smoothly. Experience shows that it is all too easy — even for the frequent exhibitor — to overlook details. You are then liable to find that you spend valuable time and nervous energy looking around for, say, drawing pins, paper and pens or trying to locate the post office or organiser's office.

The following checklist will help you to avoid last minute panics and ensure that you devote all your time to the main task of promoting your products:

1. Telephone make sure you order one, for it is essential that you can communicate with your colleagues, agents and head or branch offices. You will have to order the telephone in advance as per the organiser's instructions. In Europe and the USA, the installation arrangements are normally carried out efficiently and you can often order a telephone connection at short notice.

2. Keep a record of important telephone numbers you may need (police, security staff, medical services, exhibition organiser's office, maintenance service, etc.). Also make a note of trunk calls made (name of caller, date, time and length of call). Check the charge rates with the organisers. You will normally have to pay for installation in advance, but the invoice for calls made is obviously submitted after the exhibition has closed. Check the invoice with your records.

3. Consider locking your telephone(s): Purchase or bring suitable locks with you. It may seem unnecessary, but it is surprising how often cleaners, guards and exhibitors will try to take advantage of your phone!

4. Establish the whereabouts of post, telex and other services.

5. Local secretary: If you are far away from your offices (and especially in the case of overseas exhibitors) the employment of a local secretary is recommended. The costs are marginal and it is worth having help with appointments, dictation, refreshments and perhaps translations. Make sure you brief your secretary fully on the business and products and explain what you require done. Remember a good local secretary may also contribute valuable knowledge and contacts, especially if your stand is overseas. Ideally the secretary selected should be a native speaker with a knowledge of another language (normally English), with administrative ability and good communication and PR skills. A good secretary will be useful in developing your contacts and should be able to provide a wealth of valuable, local information.

6. Check on your insurance liabilities: If you are employing a local secretary or hostess take appropriate cover. (Normally the local contractors and organisers themselves are fully insured and you will not need to worry).

7. Stand cleaning: Arrangements vary from exhibition to exhibition and country to country. The costs of basic cleaning may be included in your rental costs. If not, get in touch with the contractors and explain what you require. For the larger stand which involves a lot of initial construction work you may need extra cleaning help to make sure your stand is really clean and tidy before opening.

8. Check that you have dusters and waste bins and that

someone is responsible for dusting and clearing rubbish away.

9. Ashtrays: Check that you have an adequate supply.

10. Fire extinguishers: Check on their availability and location. Do you know where the fire exits are in the case of an emergency?

11. Furniture: Check on the deadlines for the delivery of any furniture you may have ordered from the contractors. Make sure that the furniture is in good condition and presentable. Furniture contractors tend to give preferential treatment to their big and regular customers — beware that you do not get the 'leftovers'.

12. Lighting: Check that background and any special lighting is working properly and fitted as specified. Do you know how you can contact the contractors should you have any problems? Have you got their telephone number and a note of their working hours?

13. Check on other services (water, power supplies, etc.). Is the voltage correct for your equipment? Do you have the right plugs, etc.?

14. Maintenance: Are there arrangements for the organiser's staff to visit the stand daily to carry out minor repairs to the paintwork, lighting, partitions, etc.?

15. Exhibition passes: If you are employing contractors to carry out work on your stand, have you arranged for them to receive entrance passes?

16. Security arrangements: Check these especially if you are on a large national or collective stand. Follow security instructions and advice to the letter!

17. On-going security: If you have your own stand, weigh up the local conditions and seek advice on whether you need day and night security services. The organisers and local police will often supplement any special security arrangements you make yourself, but it would be wrong to rely on their general watchdog functions alone.

18. Packing materials: Have you considered how you will deal with empty packing cases? Are the containers properly marked? Have they been scheduled for delivery (say two days before the exhibition opens) with the forwarding agent?

19. When using a forwarding agent make sure you obtain a signature and document for the packages dispatched as these are evidence of the transfer of responsibility for delivery.

20. Refreshments: Be properly prepared for serving refreshments both to staff and visitors. If space permits and there are no buffet facilities nearby, consider hiring a refrigerator and having a dispenser for hot drinks.

21. Make sure you have (buy locally if practical) disposable glasses, plates, trays and napkins. Do you have adequate stocks of coffee, tea, sugar, snacks, beer, wine, etc?

22. Serve refreshments associated with your own country. When abroad do not attempt to offer a wide selection of specialities at the expense of basic foods and drinks. If you have to import special items, check first with the customs authorities that this is allowed.

23. Will you be using audio visual, video and similar equipment? Have you checked the electrics and do you have a spare bulb? Will you be supplying or hiring the equipment? Have you brought along the necessary transparencies, slides, videos, etc.

24. Check on your literature and display material. For overseas exhibitions take along some attractive posters with scenes of your country, miniature national flags and tourist literature.

25. Flowers: Stands can be made really attractive by hiring some flowers and plants, but make sure you have the space to display them without getting in the way of the exhibits or gangways.

26. Keep your stand looking tidy and attractive by:
- keeping coats out of sight
- keeping ashtrays clean and emptied regularly
- serving refreshments in clean cups and on clean plates
- providing waste bins and keeping refuse out of sight
- hiding parcels and boxes
- keeping your desk clear
- displaying your literature in neat piles
- keeping a notebook to record all customer enquiries and requests

27. It is best to have at least two people to man a stand — ideally you should have a marketing and a technical expert. With two (or more) people you can:
- concentrate your efforts when under pressure
- allow for breaks an dshre the workload
- plan for one (or more) of you to visit copetitors' stands
- give proper attention to each customer

28. Be prepared to advise your customers on local information such as:
- good restaurants nearby
- local entertainment
- location of the nearest bars
- location of the nearest toilets
- local transport facilities

29. Ensure your staff wear identification badges giving name, function and organisation.

11. Advertising & Public Relations

Advertising before and during the exhibition is most important for attracting buyers to your stand. You cannot rely on the exhibition organisers to do this for you. Their emphasis is on promoting the exhibition as a whole — they can do very little to promote specific exhibitors: that task is yours!

The following checklist will help you plan and execute your promotional activities:

BEFORE THE EXHIBITION

1. You need to notify existing customers and as many potential ones as possible that you plan to have a stand at the exhibition and extend an invitation to them to visit you there. It requires careful planning and resources to locate and select the most suitable list of prospective customers and media.

2. Find out where the exhibition organisers are planning to promote the exhibition.

3. Define carefully what market you are trying to reach and plan your advertising activities accordingly. If you are interested in finding agents, get in touch with the relevant agents' organisation and advertise your interest in the

periodical or circular which is sent to the membership. If you have a sophisticated product to offer and want to appeal to professional buyers, advertise in the appropriate journals. If you want to appeal to importers and whole-salers consider using direct mail geared at this market sector. Alternatively, if there is an appropriate journal which reaches this audience, consider taking space.

Reaching retailers or consumers (and perhaps the general public) requires a large press advertising budget. Exercise caution because your resources are limited. If budgets are tight you will need to consider whether you advertise in the press at all since even small adverts are expensive and unlikely to be effective. The alternative is direct promotion.

DIRECT ADVERTISING & PROMOTION

This includes sending out invitations to existing or poten-tial customers. Take care in compiling an appropriate list.

The kind of campaign you might launch could include:

1. A letter posted about two months prior to the opening date of the exhibition. Enclose a brochure listing your range of products and services highlighting any new items you will be exhibiting, with your letter. Add a prepaid postcard so that customers can easily request any addi-tional literature they require.

2. A second follow-up letter should be sent about one month before the exhibition opens. This should give details of the location and number of your stand and invite recipients to a meeting at a given date. If you organise any kind of special events (eg. a reception) send your guests a special invitation with a free entrance ticket. Come to an arrangement with the organisers, so that you only pay for the tickets actually used.

3. Organising a special event at the opening of the exhibition and inviting buyers to the exhibition are key ingredients for commercial success. You cannot only attract a lot of potential customers to your stand in this way, but also build up useful contacts and goodwill.

Such events do not have to be elaborate or call for complex preparations. A few drinks and snacks on the stand (or in an adjoining room) plus a few words of welcome by yourself or a colleagues are enough. *One week before* the exhibition send a telex reminder repeating the time, place and a telephone contact. It can pay to telephone from your stand or your hotel and confirm the meeting again: remember that important buyers tend to receive dozens of invitations like yours. If you do not chase them they may decide not to include you into their crowded schedule of engagements.

4. Preparing the advertising copy. The written material should include:

- a description of the product(s) or service(s)
- the advantages offered (eg. time-saving, efficiency, minimum maintenance, etc.)
- a list of what is new or different about your product
- special uses and applications
- key design features
- quality standards
- packaging
- price

Naturally the text should be in the appropriate language.

Your literature can serve a number of purposes eg:

- for sending to the media
- for sending to journalists
- for prospective custoemrs
- for distribution to other exhibitors

- for the exhibition organiser's Press Room or for inclusion in any daily circulation of literature such as newsletters, etc.

5. Having some photographs prepared showing individual products both in the manufacturing and finished state. Journalists welcome good literature with photographs: they tend to ignore other kinds of literature which requires detailed editing.

6. Remember that not all promotion copy needs to appear in the advertising columns. An editorial item can make a considerable impact at no charge. However, you will only attract journalists' attention if you have some interesting, innovative and attractive handout material. Provide carefully prepared copy which meets these criteria and gives specific information about your products, their benefits and applications and, if possible, comments from well-known experts and buyers in your field. Make sure you do not forget to give information about the exhibition (name, location and date) and your stand (number, location, telephone number).

Good contacts with journalists (especially for overseas exhibitions) are very important: free editorial coverage is a valuable asset. You may also like to consider taking paid space in the issue of the journal devoted to reviewing the exhibition for in that way you can reinforce your promotional message. In some instances, editorial coverage may be conditional upon taking a minimum amount of advertising space. It is always worth thinking about whether it is feasible for you to commission and place an article by an acknowledged expert in a suitable journal or magazine. This should seek to describe your products in an objective way and help to attract attention and enhance your creditability.

ACTIVITIES AT THE EXHIBITION

1. Find out from the exhibition organisers about any special events planned at the exhibition itself. Check whether there may be some events in which you can usefully participate.

2. If you decide to entertain important guests at your stand, make sure that you:

a. Inform and co-ordinate your activities with the exhibition press office
b. Arrange for a photographer to capture the handshakes and visits
c. Circulate with drinks amongst the guests (your secretary can help here)
d. Prepare your personal 'give-aways' (if appropriate)
e. Have asked that all your staff are present on the stand
f. Welcome all guests personally

The photographs can be developed quickly and published both by the local and specialised press (and back home, if it is an overseas event).

Press Conferences

3. If you have a newsworthy story (eg. special or completely new products or this is your first stand at this exhibition) it may well be worth considering holding a press conference. The advantage of press conferences is that they focus the attention of the media on your activities briefly and involve the minimum of expenditure. However, do not underestimate the amount of preparatory work required and the need to make a really professional presentation.

The smaller organisation may find the press conference too much work and of doubtful value. It is the larger organisation which is most likely to attract the media's interest. An alternative to a full press conference is simply to invite a few selected journalists (say two or three) to an interview meeting.

If you do decide on a press conference, your preparatory work needs to be precise and thoroughly planned:

a. Two weeks before the event, send written invitations to the editors or named journalists
b. Three days before the date find out who will be coming
c. Get in touch with the people who said they were coming and confirm the time and place
d. Prepare 'press folders' containing all the necessary information on your products, etc.
e. Make all the administrative arrangements for a suitable venue, refreshments, handout literature, etc.
f. Prepare yourself for journalists' questions. Think through all the possible issues which may be raised and make sure you are properly briefed to deal with them

4. There may be opportunities in some locations to screen a film on local television. You will need to explore the possibilities with the manager of the local station. If you submit your film around the time when the exhibition is being held, your film may be acceptable as a news item provided it is not simply advertising material.

Your success in this area will be dependent on the nature of your film: it will stand a chance if it is objective and factual and follows a documentary style. However, if you submit your film long before the exhibition opens, it will almost certainly be regarded as advertising material to be shown only against payment in the advertising slots.

5. Remember also the potential of local radio broadcasting. It may be worthwhile to prepare a cassette in the language of the country in which the exhibition is being held, and

send this direct to the appropriate correspondents. Make sure the material is concise and factual. Prepare yourself for dealing with requests for interviews and make sure you are fully briefed so that you can handle questions effectively: do not forget to mention the location of your stand.

6. Ensure that your organisation is properly indexed under all the appropriate headings in the exhibition catalogue. This can be an excellent advertising medium for it has a longer life than the exhibition itself and is often used by buyers as a reference work many months after the exhibition has closed.

7. Try to be selective about the way you hand out catalogues and leaflets. They are expensive and should not be readily available to casual visitors.

Seminars, Symposia & Congresses

8. At some exhibitions a programme of seminars, congresses and the like are arranged to run in parallel. If such meetings are arranged, consider whether there is some way your organisation can contribute. You or an expert colleague may be able to deliver a presentation with audio-visual materials. The lecture needs to be carefully planned and effectively delivered: ideally it should include a summary of the results of recent research and development work and refer to current trends and innovation. Make sure that a written summary is made available to delegates and that the speaker mentions your stand number, location and telephone number. The talk should link in with what you have on show and the material you have used for PR with the press.

9. Keep a tight control over your advertising activities. You need to work within the objectives you set yourself and the budget that was allocated for this purpose. Even with limited resources try not to restrict yourself to one

advertising medium. Your prospective clients are likely to read a variety of journals and you should be seeking to place adverts in a good cross section of relevant journals to make an impact. Measuring the effectiveness of advertising expenditure is always difficult, but as a general rule it is good policy to diversify the means of communication.

THE PERSONAL APPROACH

1. Your public relation activities — both before and during the exhibition — will run much more smoothly if you make personal contact with the organisers. Set up meetings with them and their advertising and PR staff. Make sure you also have good on-going contacts with editors and reporters.

2. To succeed in this area you must not be conservative. You must have creative ideas and flair, an ability to develop new angles and be aware of what the media and your market will find stimulating and newsworthy. Planning is essential but be sufficiently flexible to allow for improvisation and be ready to seize any promotional opportunities which arise. Do not forget that promotional effectiveness is not about the size of your promotion budget: it is all about achieving optimum results with a minimum of expenditure!

PRESS RELEASES

Paying attention to detail

Perhaps this is the most important aspect of your press release if you are dealing with technicalities. It must be very, very accurate.

Let us suppose that we are dealing with car engines and you have developed an accessory which will produce extra miles per gallon of petrol. In your copy to the GENERAL press it is sufficient to inform the public that the accessory is available and that it achieves X miles per gallon, with the most superficial example of the way it is achieved. But the material to a technical publication must go into the technical detail, and should contain all the non-secret data highlighting the methods by which the astonishing figure of X miles per gallon has been attained, quoting, if possible, authoritive test sources.

Any figures, data or diagramatic explanations should be double checked before committing yourself to print. There will always be an engineering genius ready to pick you up on fine points of detail that you may have accidentally overlooked. If he writes to the magazine and draws attention to it you will look foolish. More important, there is a chance that faith in your product will be lessened.

Your technical data should be preceded by an explanation in clear terms so that the reader who has an interest in engines, but doesn't necessarily have a great understanding of them, will still have his interest aroused. The reverse applies to the general press, of course.

From 'Face the Press' by James Hodge

12. Follow up Action

Following up contacts and enquiries made at an exhibition is a must. If a buyer you met at the show has to wait too long for a quotation you promised he will certainly contact other suppliers. You will have wasted your time and money and lost any goodwill you initially had. Disappointed buyers will not only hesitate to contact you again but will also talk to others in the trade and give you a bad name.

Similarly, if an enquirer at the exhibition asked for further technical information about a specific product to be sent to him and he does not receive it, you will again have lost valuable potential business and wasted time and money on your stand.

Be wary of falling into the trap of labelling some people who came to your stand as nuisances who were not worth following up. By all means use discretion and judgement, but generally speaking you should treat all exhibition enquiries seriously and worth following up.

Remember to:

1. Follow up every query immediately.

2. Write to all customers who raised any issue with you.

3. Contact all people who showed any interest or asked for further information. They may not all be immediate cus-

tomers but you should have an eye for building up longer-term goodwill.

4. Make sure you keep detailed records of all customers giving:

- Customer's name
- Function in the company
- Name of organisation
- Address
- Telephone and telex number
- Nature of the request
- Date when you responded
- Remarks and recommendations

5. Make sure you have background information on all those with whom you have not dealt with previously. Ask for details about their organisation and request a business card. As a minimum you should follow up with a catalogue or leaflet.

6. Keep a concise record of all key points made at your meetings with visitors.

7. Make sure your notes are complete and up to date. If appropriate, pass on the information to your head office or sales department on the same or the next day.

8. Do not wait till the exhibition is over but respond to buyers as soon as possible.

9. Keep up the momentum by arranging a follow up visit at the customer's offices after the exhibition is over.

10. Avoid procrastination by taking follow up action immediately if possible.

11. Invite important prospective buyers to visit your plant and offices (offer free hotel accommodation, where appropriate).

12. It is all too easy to overlook promises made at exhibitions — keep proper records and make a point of processing them urgently!

13. Remember to keep all agents or representatives fully informed of all contacts which they may be able to follow up after the exhibition.

13. Planning for Dismantling the Stand

At the end of the exhibition it is your responsibility to remove exhibits and accessories, pack them and arrange for their return. Much clearly depends on the size of your stand. If your stand is a small one and you are using your own staff and vehicles, make sure everyone is briefed on their duties. If you have a large stand with outside contractors and forwarding agents involved, make sure they have all been properly instructed.

You will need to make sure that the following points are effectively dealt with:

1. Before the exhibition check that everything has been properly packed, marked correctly and that all the necessary paperwork is on order. For overseas exhibitions be especially careful to get the correct export documentation prepared. All this will help you later when it comes to checking items after dismantling the stand.

2. Keep empty packing cases. Check where they are stored so that you can readily locate them when it comes to packing up.

3. In the case of overseas exhibitions:

a. It is particularly important to invite the customs and shipping agent to your stand one day before the exhibition closes. If you wish to leave some items behind (perhaps for customers) check that this will be done. Get the necessary paperwork prepared. This must include an exact description of the products in each parcel and their value. It is important that the total value of all goods being shipped home should equal the value of goods originally brought into the country.

b. Remember that overseas exhibitions are treated as though they were bonded warehouses: thus all products on show are exempt from import duties provided they are shipped back to the country of origin.

c. You will also need to fix a time and date for packing with the customs or shipping agent. You must be there during the packing process paying special attention to any fragile and sensitive items. If necessary pack or supervise the packing of delicate items personally. Make sure that the original packing materials have been retained and are available on the stand when the exhibition closes. Order some extra packing material, if necessary, and make sure you have suitable packing and binding tape and tools on hand. All packing cases should be marked clearly on at least two sides.

4. In the case of domestic shows or exhibitions make sure that you have made (and had confirmed) all the arrangements for dismantling, packing, freight, etc. This may involve not only your own staff, but perhaps also staff recruited for the duration of the exhibition only ie. contractors, haulage firms, electricians, etc.

5. When the documents are ready and the products packed, ask the shipping agent for a written confirmation that the merchandise is now his responsibility. Do not just leave your products or the exhibition centre before obtaining such confirmation.

6. See to it that no personal effects are included in the consignment to be returned.

To ensure your Company's smooth pull-out from the Exhibition, we ask that certain information be passed to members of your staff who will be involved in the removal of your exhibits.

1. The Exhibition closes at 16.00 hrs on Wednesday, 30th March. No exhibits or displays may be dismantled or removed from the hall before this time as it is both discourteous to visitors and other Exhibitors and contrary to contract. The Exhibition security staff have been instructed to stop any exhibits leaving the building before this time.

2. General dismantling of the Exhibition may commence at 16.05 on Wednesday, 30th March. All exhibits and displays MUST be clear of the hall by 22.00 hrs. on this day. You may find it advantageous to bring in a trolley for your dismantling - TROLLEYS ARE NOT AVAILABLE FOR HIRE ON SITE.

3. Catering equipment, furniture, flowers etc., which have been hired remain the responsibility of the Exhibitor until such times as they are returned to the sources from which they were obtained.

4. Please collect your remaining Press Kits from the Press Centre on the ground floor.

5. Standfitting and electrical material must be cleared by 16.00 hrs. on Thursday, 31st March.

Example of Stand Dismantling Timetable

7. Check receipt of the packing cases and products on your return.

8. If you should discover any damaged or short shipments, notify your Insurance Company or Brokers without delay.

14. Feedback information during and after the Exhibition

You should throughout an exhibition be thinking about what information to pass back to your head office, factory or warehouse. You will also certainly need to liaise with colleagues over queries, prices, delivery dates, etc. Make sure you have a detailed list and telephone numbers so that you can easily make contact. In the case of overseas exhibitions make sure you allow for time differentials and check before the exhibition that the appropriate colleagues will be available if necessary.

You should also be keeping simple records and statistics so that when the exhibition is over you have basic data to include in your reports to management.

The following checklist will help you to be properly prepared:

1. Report any special events during the exhibition to your company: some of your colleagues will be expecting reports and feedback. Send photographs and a summary of highlights for the press.

2. Pre-arrange times — say twice a day (morning and evening) — when you can best communicate with your offices to deal with any urgent matters. In the case of

distant overseas exhibitions do not forget the time differences!

3. Remember that you will in part have to rely on staff back at your offices. Check that key staff will be available to respond quickly with any urgent queries you may have. Ensure that you receive clear and full replies regarding prices, delivery terms and dates, etc.

4. Make it a rule to respond to all buyers' queries, etc., within one week of returning to home base.

5. Aim to prepare an 'Exhibition Results Report' and also a report of all expenditure incurred no later than two weeks after the exhibition closure.

6. Most exhibition organisers will automatically send you a post exhibition report. If you do not receive a report, ask for them to let you have one which gives facts and figures of numbers and breakdowns of visitors, etc.

7. Buy and retain the exhibition catalogue for future reference.

8. Send copies of any interesting catalogues and other information you have collected from exhibitors back to your headquarters.

9. Obtain the following quantative data:
a. Number of orders obtained (quantity and value)
b. Number of new contacts made with prospective cus-
    tomers (give names and summarise their main areas of
    interest, etc.)
c. Summarise customers' queries and comments on your
    products and packaging
d. Number of visitors to your stand by suitable break-
    downs, eg.
    Importers
    Wholesalers

Retailers
Professions, etc.
e. Summarise meetings with agents (eg. their opinions, specific suggestions for increasing sales, etc).
f. Number of overseas customers who you met and will follow up
g. Total Actual and Budget exhibition expenditure
h. Report any other quantative information which is relevant
i. Report on information such as advertising effectiveness, new contacts made, competitors' activities, etc.

10. Remember that the information you collect and transmit to your management will determine whether you participate in next year's exhibition. Obviously the final decision may be influenced by a number of factors, but it is important to include the number of actual orders received or new business generated. This can only accurately be assessed a few months after the exhibition has closed since it clearly takes time for some business to emerge as firm orders.

15. Exhibition Visitor's Questionnaire

Many exhibition organisers carry out surveys to measure how successful an exhibition or fair has been. The following are examples of the kind of questions asked. It is unlikely that individual exhibitors will find it worthwhile to conduct their own detailed survey of visitors to their stand. However, there may be special circumstances where such an exercise is deemed necessary.

Before considering a postal survey remember that they require quite a lot of know-how on designing questionnaires, phrasing questions correctly, deciding who to send them to and planning how to analyse the replies. It is normally well worthwhile to ask the organisers of your exhibition whether they have conducted or commissioned a survey.

Get hold of a copy. It may be a relatively simple report based on an analysis of the information provided on the registration forms. Alternatively it is sometimes a more detailed survey which provides data supplied as a result of postal questionnaires and perhaps even some personal interviews with a representative cross-section of visitors.

No matter what type of report, they all provide useful information which should help you to evaluate your own company's exhibition performance. For example, do your own records (and impressions) on the number of (say) overseas visitors tally with the information contained in the report?

If there are major discrepancies on this and other features why should this be? What can you learn from the data? Can you use any of the general information provided in the exhibition organisers' report in your own report to management? How does the overall data compare with your own?

1. Did you visit the exhibition last year?   YES   NO
Did you visit the exhibition 2 years ago?   YES   NO

2. What are your prime reasons for visiting the exhibition this year?

3. How many hours did you spend at the exhibition eg.:
Monday .... hours
Tuesday .... hours
Wednesday .... hours

4. Your organisation's country of origin and home-town or city ....

5. Which three stands at the exhibition impressed you the most? Please give brief reasons: eg.
Company.   Stand No.   Display.   Product.   Literature.
Design.   Staff.

6. Which products or services interested you the most?

7. As a result of the exhibition have you decided to:
Recommend the purchase of equipment, etc.?
Place an order?
Locate local suppliers?
Other? (please specify).

8. What is the total value of orders placed as a result of your visit this year?

9. How much have you been allocated to spend on the purchase of the following products or services in the coming 12 months?

10. Did you find the exhibition useful to you?   YES   NO

11. What promotion activity prompted you to attend?

12. Which trade or professional journal(s) do you normally read?

13. Do you go to the exhibition with the intention of placing orders OR
Do you prefer exhibitors to contact you after the exhibition is over?

An analysis of questions such as these (and many others) will help you to establish, for example:

1. Percentage of visiting decision-makers.

2. Breakdown of visitors by countries and major commercial centres.

3. Average number of hours visitors spend at the exhibition.

4. Key reasons for visiting.

5. Number of visitors likely to place orders.

6. An indication of future purchasing plans.

7. Breakdown of visitors by size and function.

8. An overview of other exhibitors:
   Why do they attend?
   Will they take space in the next exhibition?
   Were they satisfied with the organisation, etc?

9. Total number of exhibition visitors compared with visitors to your stand.

Other information you should collect after the exhibition is over:

1. Which products attracted interest and by whom?

2. Value of orders placed at the exhibition.

3. Number of visitors requesting further meetings in their offices or yours.

4. Did you come across any items which could be useful in developing new products?

5. Did you obtain any useful advice or information from professional visitors to your stand (eg. engineers, designers, etc.)?

6. Did you make useful business contacts with other exhibitors (perhaps in order to co-operate in production or marketing activities)?

7. On the strength of your experience, do you intend to exhibit at other exhibitions in the next two years?

8. Do you have detailed records of enquiries and orders received from overseas visitors? How will you exploit these opportunities?

9. What did you find to be the most effective advertising and promotion activities? Have you kept a record of appropriate local publications and their circulation?

10. Can you quantify the amount of new business built up as a direct result of the exhibition?

11. What effect has there been on home and export sales since the exhibition closed? Can you identify new business achieved (say) six months after the exhibition?

When finally all the hectic days of the exhibition are over you should make a point of having a day off to recover and hopefully celebrate your success. It is only the foolhardy who attempt to go straight back to work the following day. Exhibitions are tiring and stressful occasions and involve long hours of activity.

First, before you go off to relax and take a well-earned rest, check that you have settled any outstanding payments which may be due to electricians, local staff, suppliers, cleaners and shipping agents, etc.

Second, make a point of thanking all those who have helped you plan and run your stand — your staff, the organisers, contractors, etc. In appropriate cases you may wish to show your appreciation with a token gift.

16. Further Reading

GENERAL:
Data Book for Exhibitions, Trade Fairs and Conference Centres.
Information Services, East Grinstead, W. Sussex.

Provides a comprehensive guide to about 1,800 UK and European exhibitions and trade fairs listed alphabetically under broad subject areas. Also lists exhibition and conference centres geographically by country, stand contractors, travel consultants, interpreters, etc. Quarterly supplements with updated information.

Exhibitions — the Marketing Challenge
Unibrand Training, London.

Free booklet highlighting problems posed by participating in an exhibition and suggests some of the solutions. Outlines ways of evaluating exhibition performances against other promotion activities.

NEGOTIATING:
Negotiating Profitable Sales
John Lidstone, Gower, Farnborough, 221 pp.

Practical guide to successful business negotiations in the consumer product field with specimen dialogues, negotiating techniques and checklists.

Getting to Yes
Roger Fisher and William Ury, Hutchinson, London, 161 pp.

Based on Harvard University research into negotiations. The message is to stick to reasonable behaviour, resist pressure and avoid tricks. The best negotiations succeed because of integrity!

PUBLIC RELATIONS:

Face the Press
James Hodge, Management Update, Shrewsbury, 135 pp.

Aimed at the small and medium sized company. Advice on promoting and projecting the activities of a business via the press and PR. Explains what the press is looking for and how to prepare Press Releases and run successful press conferences.

The Practice of Public Relations
Wilfred Howard (Editor), Heinemann, London, 250 pp.

Fifteen practitioners explain how they tackle different aspects of PR. Advice of using different types of media, timing of press releases, etc.

AGENTS:

Export Agents
Colin McMillan and Sydney Paulden, Gower, Farnborough 237 pp.

Explains different kinds of agency and shows how to select a suitable one for your business. Includes specimen contracts, problems of dealing with agents in different countries, etc.

Succeeding as a Manufacturers' Agent
G. J. Robinson, Management Update, Shrewsbury, 142 pp.

Step by step guide to setting up as a self-employed agent. Advice on drawing up contracts, agency law in Europe, etc.

A useful training film by Video Arts 'How not to exhibit yourself' deals with the basics of running an effective exhibition stand. (30 mins running time) available in 16mm and film and video formats.